navigate

UNDERSTANDING & PURSUING GOD'S WILL

NAVIGATE. Copyright © 2014 by DiscipleGuide Church Resources. All rights reserved. No part of this publication may be reproduced or transmitted in any form or by any means, electronic or mechanical, including photocopy, recording, or any information storage and retrieval system, without permission in writing from the publisher. Requests for permission to make copies of any part of this work should be mailed to: Permissions, DiscipleGuide Church Resources, PO Box 1749, Conway, AR 72033.

ISBN 978-0-89114-515-8

Unless otherwise indicated, all Scripture quotations are from The Holy Bible, English Standard Version® (ESV®), copyright © 2001 by Crossway, a publishing ministry of Good News Publishers. Used by permission. All rights reserved.

Scripture quotations marked (NKJV) are from the New King James Version®. Copyright © 1982 by Thomas Nelson, Inc. Used by permission. All rights reserved.

Printed in the United States of America

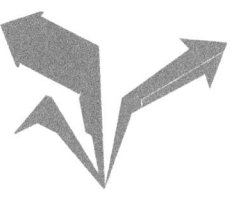

Contents

WHAT IS GOD'S WILL?	5
GOD'S WILL IS IN HIS WORD	21
GOD'S WILL IS IN WISDOM	47
GOD'S WILL IS IN WORSHIP	69

WHAT IS GOD'S WILL?

Have you ever struggled to determine "God's will for your life"? Have you spent sleepless nights agonizing over decisions, afraid you might miss out on "God's best"? Have you ever explained a major life change as "God's will" — then later changed your mind?

Does God really intend for us to be confused about how to please Him?

I don't think so.

Mixed Signals?

Jennifer can't wait to tell friends at school her news: "Tim asked me out on a date. I feel like

God has been leading me to him for months. This must be confirmation!"

Two months later, Jennifer and Tim break up. Tim says it's God's will.

Did God send Jennifer the wrong message?

Craig sits down with his parents during a weekend home from college. "I feel like God is moving me to change my major from business to art," he explains.

A semester later, Craig informs his parents that God is telling him to pursue a degree in computer science.

Is God leading Craig on a wild goose chase?

Late one night, unable to sleep, Jim flips through television channels and sees a tourism ad for California. The next morning, Jim announces to his boss, "I'm resigning. God gave me a sign, and I'm supposed to move to California."

Weeks later, Jim calls his boss and asks if his old position is still available. There are no jobs to be found in California, Jim says, and he's just never felt at peace there.

Is God playing games with Jim's career?

Just listening to all the leading, guiding, telling, moving, and directing that God gets credit for, it sure seems like He's grown fickle these days.

But was all that really from God?

Defining Terms

As we explore God's will, let's start with some basics.

First, passages such as Mark 3:35, Romans 8:27, Romans 12:2, 1 Corinthians 1:1, and many others refer specifically to *"the will of God."* So yes, God does indeed have a will.

Scripture portrays different aspects of this will of His. In verses such as Ephesians 1:1, we see God's *sovereign will* at work. This includes decrees God has made that cannot be changed — such as His plan to send Jesus to die on the cross.

God's *moral will* refers to that which pleases Him (as seen in passages such as Ephesians 5:17; 1 Thessalonians 4:3-7; 5:18; 1 Peter 3:17). The Ten Commandments are also a great example. Jesus summed up God's moral will in words quoted from the Old Testament: *"You shall love the Lord your God with all your heart and with all your soul and with all your mind,"* and *"You shall love your neighbor as yourself"* (Matthew 22:37-39).[1]

Finally, Scripture portrays God's *directive will* as He guides a person's life. This is what most people have in mind when they speak of "God's will." In Genesis 12:1-2, God communicates His personal, directive will for Abraham by telling him to pack up his family and leave his homeland. Many Christians are looking for the same type of communication from God today — some "sign" or "word" telling them to "go left," "go right," "stay put," "take that job," "marry this person," or "sell that stock now."

While it's helpful to identify these various aspects of God's will, in the grand scheme of eternity they all work together under His authority to perfectly achieve His purposes.

Controlling Traffic

In large cities, traffic is often monitored and controlled from a central office. Behind the "Authorized Personnel Only" door, controllers watch screens displaying current images and data from traffic cameras and sensors. When they notice congestion building up, they can change the traffic flow in several ways. They may alter how long certain traffic lights stay red or green. Or they may dictate a warning to flash on a roadside message board, instructing drivers to take a detour. When accidents occur, the traffic controllers help direct emergency personnel in responding to the scene.

When these things happen, the controllers don't take time to explain why the red light you're stopped at on Main Street is suddenly longer, or why there's a detour around Third and Washington, or where they're sending those emergency vehicles that just zipped by you. Taking time to explain all that to everyone would only cause more delays.

Can you imagine what would happen if people stopped trusting this system? Just think of the chaos if everyone started pulling into intersections whenever they had a "hunch" the light should change. Or what if everyone, out of curiosity, started racing behind the emergency vehicles they see speeding to an accident scene?

As drivers, we aren't promised to be kept informed of everything that's happening throughout the traffic grid — instead, we're simply instructed to follow the rules and directions laid out in our state driver's manual. That manual tells us to go on green and stop on red. It explains who goes first at a four-way stop. It gives directions on how closely to follow other vehicles and how to determine when it's safe to pass. Meanwhile, as we follow the manual, the controllers work behind the scenes to help us get where we're going. Our obedience to the manual ensures that we react correctly in any scenario the controllers use to direct us.

That's what God's will is like. We aren't privy to everything happening behind the scenes. Instead, we acknowledge God's control of it all, and as long as we obey His written Word (our manual), we can trust Him to work all things for the good of those who love him and are called according to his purpose (Romans 8:28). Our duty, then, is to obey the revelation we've been given.

Although helpful, this illustration has its limits as a picture of God's will. While a traffic controller works with a team of people to monitor events, God already knows everything about everything everywhere at all times — without any help. And while a controller reacts to events, God is proactive, already guiding the future before it happens. Further, whereas traffic controllers are limited to merely placing information in front of people to guide them, God has power to change our hearts and minds.

Most importantly, unlike traffic controllers who are imperfect, God is perfect and sovereignly works all things at the same time perfectly (though we rarely notice His divine intervention). He never has to "redirect traffic" because of any decisions of ours that He wasn't expecting. Somehow, in His unfathomable wisdom, He has already made our decisions a part of His perfect plan. In fact, in His perfect knowledge, God never needs any kind of "control room" to monitor any situation here on earth.

God has instructed us to obey His manual, the Bible. That's our assignment in pursuing His will. While He uses various other means (circumstances, events, our desires, etc.) to direct us, He doesn't let us see everything from His "behind the scenes" perspective. God has chosen to keep certain matters to himself — which is why it's never profitable for you or me to spend time trying to figure out those things.

Navigate

In other words, we are called to *navigate* God's will by obeying the traffic rules of life given by the One who rules life's traffic. In this way, God accomplishes His will through our obedience and His divine intervention.

Off Limits

In the Old Testament, the man Job was reprimanded by God for speculating on such behind-the-scenes information. Job was miserable after suffering the loss of his possessions, his children, and his health. Although at first he honored God in the midst of his suffering, eventually he *"opened his mouth and cursed the day of his birth. And Job said: 'Let the day perish on which I was born'"* (Job 3:1-3).

It was like telling God, "I don't trust you anymore. If I was in control, I would have done things differently and better. But because You, God, have messed everything up for me, I'd rather not have been born."

Eventually God responded by asking a series of questions to reveal Job's inadequacy. Here's a sample:

> Where were you when I laid the foundation of the earth?
> Tell me, if you have understanding.
> Who determined its measurements — surely you know!
> Or who stretched the line upon it?
> On what were its bases sunk,
> or who laid its cornerstone,
> when the morning stars sang together
> and all the sons of God shouted for joy?
> (Job 38:4-7).

This goes on for thirty-four more verses! And it sent a clear message to Job: "You can't handle the kind of information you're dabbling with. It's off limits."

Finally, Job admitted that God's purposes were unstoppable and too wonderful to explain:

> Then Job answered the Lord and said:
> "I know that you can do all things,
>   and that no purpose of yours can be thwarted.…
> I have uttered what I did not understand,
>   things too wonderful for me, which I did not know" (Job 42:1-3).

Job learned not just to accept that God keeps some things hidden from us, but to rejoice that some things were *"too wonderful"* for him (verse 3). As John Calvin advised, when God "closes his holy mouth, we should desist from inquiry."[2]

But that doesn't mean we can't learn more about God. In fact, He reveals Himself to us in several ways.

How God Reveals Himself

God's *natural revelation* is found in every man's heart (Romans 1:19). It communicates that God exists and that He demands righteousness and judges wickedness. This revelation isn't enough to save us (since it gives no details about Christ), but it is sufficient to condemn human beings for their rebellion against God.

Biblical revelation refers to God's communication through His Word. God has spoken through prophets, through apostles, and through Jesus, who is the Word made flesh. This revelation has been recorded for us in God's written Word (Hebrews 1:1-2; 2 Peter 1:21).

God's *special revelation* refers to His direct communication to human beings, apart from His written Word — such as through visions, dreams, angel messengers, and even His audible voice. Often today, when people claim God is leading, guiding, directing, or moving them to do something, they're essentially claiming *special revelation*.

Although God is free to use any method whatsoever to speak to us, He has chosen to do so by the Spirit through His Word. The message of this book is simple: Knowing the will of God is rooted in obeying His written Word — *not* seeking special revelation apart from His Word.

Sadly Misinformed

But that doesn't mean people searching for special revelation are necessarily first-degree heretics. They're usually sincere followers of Christ who, while well intentioned, are sadly misinformed through various misconceptions about God's will.

One common misconception envisions God's will as a tightrope where one wrong move could ruin your life and require you to start all over again — or worse, to be kept eternally out of God's will. This view assumes God is powerless to work through our faults. But, it's a view that has a difficult time explaining how God could choose a first-degree murderer like Moses (Exodus 2:11-12) to lead His people out of Egypt, or how someone like Peter could preach powerfully at Pentecost (Acts 2:14-41) only months after Jesus rebuked him and called him *"Satan"* (Matthew 16:23). God, it seems, isn't wringing His hands over imperfect people who could mess up His will.

A variation of this error over-emphasizes the *perfect* will of God as something we're obligated to strive for. According to this view, as we consider the range of possible choices confronting us, we're supposed to recognize that "our main goal should be to hit God's bull's-eye"[3] and nothing less.

A much different but equally misleading viewpoint is the open-door theory of God's will. Some people are ready to believe that *any* opportunity rising up before them must be from God. They quote (totally out of context) Revelation 3:8 — *"I have set before you an open door, which no one is able to shut."* But *which* door? If we're honest, we recognize that most situations in life present multiple options and possibilities.

Perhaps the most popular misconception regarding God's will is the follow-your-heart theory, a spiritualized version of the most dominant philosophy in today's anything-goes culture. Eager to receive divine guidance, many people start believing that their every hunch or feeling must be God's way of trying to tell them something. But the big problem here is that *"the heart is deceitful above all things, and desperately sick; who can understand it?"* (Jeremiah 17:9).

Moreover, many of the feelings people interpret as divine nudgings are only an emotional reaction to difficult circumstances they'd like to escape. Like Jonah stumbling upon a boat bound for Tarshish, opportunities can seem providential when they link easily with our selfish longings.

Not How It Should Be

And so, in our search for God's guidance, we either end up stressed out from trying to stay on the tightrope or hit the bull's-eye — or else bewildered by the uncertainty of multiple open doors and the torrent of our fickle, ever-changing feelings. We wonder: *Will God's will always be dangling just outside our reach?*

The whole thing gets so confusing! And it seems at odds with the encouragement we hear in Christ's promises: *"My yoke is easy, and my burden is light"* (Matthew 11:30); *"Ask, and it will be given to you; seek, and you will find; knock, and it will be opened to you"* (Luke 11:9).

How can we escape the confusion and take hold of a more encouraging perspective?

Where do we go to truly find God's will?

NOTES

1. Scripture quotations in this book, unless otherwise noted, are from *The Holy Bible, English Standard Version®* (ESV®), copyright © 2001 by Crossway, a publishing ministry of Good News Publishers. Used by permission. All rights reserved.

2. John Calvin, *Commentaries on the Epistle of Paul the Apostle to the Romans,* translated by John Owen (Grand Rapids, Michigan: Baker Book House, 2003), 354.

3. Haddon Robinson, *Decision-Making by the Book* (Wheaton, Illinois: Victor Books, 1991), 21.

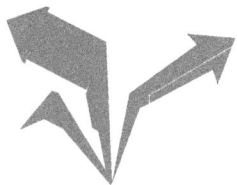

GOD'S WILL IS IN HIS WORD

In the ancient world, as people sought direction from their gods, they would sometimes cut open animals and closely watch the motion of the intestines as they spilled out. Through these movements, they believed, the gods were communicating direction for them. These people were trying to navigate via a *gut feeling*, you might say.[1]

Others down through history have sought divine guidance by looking upward to the motion of stars and planets; on your birthday, certain alignments of these heavenly bodies were considered to bring either good or ill fortune.

Still others have looked for divine words of

guidance as conjured up by certain specialists — mediums, spiritists, diviners, or sorcerers.[2] But God, in the Old Testament, repeatedly commands His children not to consult such persons (Leviticus 19:31; 20:6, 27; Deuteronomy 18:9-14).

Today, most Christians would not dare consult a psychic or clairvoyant. But they commit a similar sin every time they try to get an "inside track" on the secret mind of God.

"The secret things belong to the LORD our God," we read in Deuteronomy 29:29, *"but the things that are revealed belong to us and to our children forever, that we may do all the words of this law."* The things God *has* chosen to reveal are certainly for our benefit as we obey. Yet the vast majority of His infinite knowledge is off limits for us. (Our little brains couldn't handle it anyway: *"For who has known the mind of the Lord…?"* — Romans 11:34.) If, however, we continually act as if we deserve to know divine mysteries, we become like little children who think they're entitled to know every detail of mom and dad's bank accounts and refuse to be happy with the generous allowance they've been given.

While it's admirable to seek more intimate knowledge of God, we must be careful to avoid dangerous assumptions, such as thinking we're entitled to know whatever God knows, or that He hasn't revealed enough in His Word, or that He's being less than kind or less than honest by hiding His will from us.

Martin Luther put it this way: "We must keep in view his word and leave alone his inscrutable will; for it is by his word and not by his inscrutable will that we must be guided."[3]

The further we move away from trusting Scripture, the more dangerous our thinking becomes.

The Greatest Treasure

The most important reason we should cling to what God has revealed in His Word is that God Himself places priority on it. As David acknowledged, *"You have exalted above all things your name and your word"* (Psalm 138:2).

The process God ordained to provide us with His Word involved a great deal of time and vast resources. Over a span of 1,500 years, He used forty human authors to pen His Word perfectly. That is no light task. The Bible is our most valuable treasure on earth, and to insist on receiving special revelation beyond and apart from it communicates a lack of understanding and appreciation for the weight of Scripture.

Many act as if the Bible's preface reads, "To whom it may concern: Good luck — you'll need it." — As if God is playing a cruel game of hide-and-seek with us.

Instead, Paul tells us, *"All Scripture is breathed out by God and profitable for teaching, for reproof, for correction, and for training in righteousness, that the man of God may be complete, equipped for every good work"* (2 Timothy 3:16-17). The implications here are momentous, as Wayne Grudem points out:

> It is in Scripture alone that we search for God's words to us. And we should, eventually, arrive at contentment with what we find there. The sufficiency of Scripture should encourage us to search through the Bible to try to find what God would have us think about a certain issue

or do in a certain situation. Everything that God wants to tell all his people for all time about that kind of issue or situation will be found on the pages of the Bible. While the Bible might not directly answer every question we can think up — for "the secret things belong to the LORD our God" (Deut. 29:29) — it will provide us with the guidance we need "for every good work" (2 Tim. 3:17).[4]

God's Word is a gift that frees us from the burden of struggling to discover God's will through unsure means.

More Sure

Think for a moment about how familiar the apostle Peter must have been with the voice of Jesus, after walking at His side for three years. Moreover, Peter also knew what the voice of the Father sounded like, for he heard it sounding forth from heaven when Jesus was transfigured (Matthew 17:4-6). But when Peter later recalls this experience, he says there's something "more sure" than the audible voice of God: His written Word

(2 Peter 1:17-21). What a bold statement!

Commenting on this passage and its exalted view of Scripture, Jonathan Edwards asked, "Why should anyone desire a higher kind of intercourse with heaven…?"[5] And yet so many people do.

I know a lot of people who claim they've received guidance from God in the form of a mysterious feeling. And I'm aware that some people even claim to have heard the audible voice of God. Everyone seems to agree that God's audible voice is weightier than subjective feelings, and yet, according to Peter's teaching, Scripture supersedes them both. Peter's logic leads us to believe that we can place more confidence in God's written Word than in His audible voice!

While that may sound strange, it makes perfect sense. As an example, one of my most treasured possessions is a Father's Day card my wife, Jill, wrote to me when we were expecting. She wrote it from our unborn son's perspective and signed it, "Baby."

Three months after our son, Bryce, was born, Jill passed away. In fifty years, I will still be able to read those precious words just as she wrote them. However, I have already forgotten the verbal words she spoke to me that special day. If it is that difficult to be confident in a verbal message, can you imagine how difficult it would be to remain confident in a subjective feeling after years have passed?

This is even more true when comparing the Scriptures with any subjective feelings that we look to for divine guidance. In their book *Guidance and the Voice of God,* Phillip Jensen and Tony Payne make this point:

> Time and again, God urges us through the Scriptures to listen to his word, to attend to the public reading and teaching of Scripture, to study and meditate upon Scripture, to gaze intently into what it says and then do it. But nowhere does he urge to us to seek signs, visions, dreams, still small voices, and such things.[6]

One reason this is true is the vast difference in reliability between written words and the more subjective impressions such as feelings and dreams. Written words are *objective,* in the sense of bearing a specific message as determined by the writer.

If the written instructions for a new piece of ready-to-assemble furniture tell us to use a screwdriver for a certain step, we know that doesn't mean to pick up a sledgehammer instead. If Scripture says, "Love others," we can't mistake that for "Hate others"; it's written clearly for all to see.

On the other hand, our feelings and experiences are much more *subjective* and highly susceptible to varying interpretations. If a mother gives a strange look toward her children, one child may think Mom looks displeased, another may suppose she's deep in thought, while another may interpret the look as anxious and confused.

That's why Scripture alone is the only source of revelation we can be completely confident in. While we might disagree on what God means in various passages, we can't disagree on the content of the passage itself. Instead of relying on man's interpretation, God's Word stands on its own authority.

An Issue of Faith

So why are we tempted to pursue subjective feelings and ignore Scripture? Why are we so caught up in the mysterious that we miss the obvious?

I think it boils down to a lack of faith.

Faith requires us to let go of our own understanding and trust God: *"Trust in the L*ORD* with all your heart, and do not lean on your own understanding"* (Proverbs 3:5). The problem is, we love our own understanding (Proverbs 14:12). That's why it's so appealing to follow our feelings.

"Faith comes from hearing," we read in Romans 10:17, *"and hearing through the word of Christ."* Faith, we could say, is always built upon God's Word. But that's a difficult proposition for many who either don't want to take time to study Scripture, or are disgruntled because they can't find information in the Bible dealing with a specific issue in their lives (a job choice, for example, or a decision about moving somewhere). Of course, they could seek wisdom and discernment from the principles of Scripture — but then that would require (you guessed it) faith.

Many want a peek into the future in order to avoid difficult circumstances and suffering. But if we avoid future difficulties, we won't develop wisdom and character (Romans 5:3-4). This kind of thinking is self-motivated, not Christ-motivated. All parents want their children to grow in their ability to make decisions based upon knowledge, experience, and wisdom, and to act and speak with integrity and uprightness. Where does this parental desire come from? I believe it stems from the image of God, who also wants His children to develop decision-making skills that reflect His wisdom and to live out that wisdom in all areas of life.

But if we keep acting according to our feelings as shaped by our own understanding, how will we ever be transformed to be more Christlike? Instead, we'll only grow more *me*-like.

God's Word exposes our feelings for what they really are. Hebrews 4:12 explains it: *"For the word of God is living and active, sharper than any two-edged sword, piercing to the division of soul and of spirit, of joints and of marrow, and discerning the thoughts and intentions of the heart."*

Think about the remarkable change this points to: When we read God's Word, we look to God while His Word "reads" our hearts! It exposes our sin, and awakens our desire to follow Christ. That's a total transformation!

"But wait," you might say. "Doesn't all this talk about the Word bypass the role of the Holy Spirit?" Absolutely not. Remember, God's Word is described in Ephesians 6 as *"the sword of the Spirit."* The Word takes on the Spirit's power:

> By his Spirit, God unstops our deaf ears and opens our blind eyes, and as the words of the Bible come to our minds, we experience an extraordinary thing — we realize with a shattering certainty that we are not simply reading words on a page, or listening to some nonentity speak; God himself is speaking to us.[7]

God the Holy Spirit inspired men to write Scripture (2 Peter 1:21). So why would He suddenly bypass Scripture and communicate in some other way? As theologian and counselor Jay Adams observes, "It is absurd to suppose that the Spirit would spend years producing the Scriptures only to circumvent them regularly by resorting to other methods of guiding believers."[8]

It All Comes Back to the Word

Others may ask, "Doesn't God use circumstances to guide us? Shouldn't the counsel of fellow Christians have a role? Doesn't prayer have a role in decision-making?"

Of course, it's absolutely true that God gives us desires and places us in circumstances in order to guide us. But based on these things we can easily make conclusions that go too far. There are too many possibilities and factors beyond our small understanding for us to safely say, "I totally see what God is up to."

For instance, you might receive a strong desire to share the gospel. Did that come from God? Of course. It's scriptural. It's always completely appropriate to say, "God wants me to share the gospel."

At the same time, suppose you hear that a former teacher of yours is deathly ill in the hospital, and you're quite certain he doesn't know Jesus. Can you now safely say, "I know what God is up to. He's set this whole thing up for me to share the gospel with my teacher"? While this is a possibility, you still can't make that claim with certainty.

That would be assuming to know all the same information God knows. After all, only God can tell the future.

You *could* say, "I know God is pleased with my desire to evangelize my teacher," but you must stop short of claiming that it has been decreed by God since before time began. After all, what if your teacher dies before you can make it to the hospital? Did God see that coming? Of course He did. But *you* didn't.

That's why we must be careful about putting words in God's mouth. Otherwise we're claiming that, like God, we know and control every detail of every situation in the universe. The biblical approach is rather to take biblical commands (such as our responsibility to share the gospel with everyone) and then to make decisions based upon them. Our confidence is not in the fact that we *know* exactly what God is doing, but that *God* knows what He's doing.

In the situation with your hospitalized teacher, it could be God was planning for you to arrive at the hospital after your teacher died, and then have an opportunity to share the gospel with the entire family. Or it could be something else entirely different. The point is, God is much more creative than we are. When we start assuming we know what He's up to, we immediately try to bring Him down to our level. But God says, *"My thoughts are not your thoughts, neither are your ways my ways, declares the LORD"* (Isaiah 55:8).

George Whitefield, a bold evangelist of the Great Awakening, found himself in the midst of just such an unexpected detour. While his wife was pregnant, George began to make grand predictions about his unborn son's life — including the time of his birth. He even predicted that his son would be another great evangelist. However, in early 1744, George Whitfield discovered the error of making such predictions when his infant son died.

> I hope that what happened before his birth, and since his death, hath taught me such lessons, as, if duly improved, may render his mistaken parent more cautious, more sober minded, more experienced in Satan's devices, and consequently more useful in his future labors the church of God.... Not doubting but our

future life will be one continued explanation of this blessed riddle, I commend myself and you to the unerring guidance of God's Word and Spirit.[9]

Painfully, Whitfield admitted his error in listening to the voice of Satan rather than trusting the Word of God. *"And no wonder, for even Satan disguises himself as an angel of light"* (2 Corinthians 11:14).

Although Scripture never indicates that we're entitled to a full explanation for why we have certain desires or are placed in certain circumstances, we can be confident that God is achieving His purposes through them. *"The heart of man plans his way, but the LORD establishes his steps"* (Proverbs 16:9). *"The king's heart is a stream of water in the hand of the LORD; he turns it wherever he will"* (Proverbs 21:1).

Behind the Scenes

Occasionally, Scripture gives us glimpses of the secret workings in God's "control room." For instance, Exodus 7:3 makes it clear that God hardened the heart of Pharaoh; in 2 Corinthians 8:16 we read how God gave Titus a desire to care for the Corinthians; and Joshua 24:12 reveals how God sent hornets to drive out the two kings of the Amorites on Joshua's behalf.

Here is where we find the two sides of navigation intersecting: The same one who has given us the traffic rules also rules the traffic. Knowing that God is working providentially behind the scenes to accomplish his will gives us even more confidence to trust His Word. The wise navigator knows that God will never allow His divine working to contradict His Word.

Every event, occurrence, desire, and thought — they all operate entirely under God's sovereign control. "There are no maverick *molecules* running around loose," as R. C. Sproul puts it.[10] Now, add to that the fact that God is working perfectly through all things everywhere, all at once. It's not as if He works in Joe's life for a few days, then moves to Carla's life for a while, and then turn his attention to Bill's life. No, everything God does works perfectly toward fulfilling His perfect plan for everyone at all times.

Whether you've realized it or not, God has been sovereign over your life even before you entered this world. He chose your birthday, your birthplace, your birth-parents, and countless other details about your life — all the way down to your exact genetic make-up.

God's sovereignty over all these things reminds me of Scrabble. Occasionally I can get a triple-word-score. And when my game is really on, I can spell words horizontally and vertically all in the same move!

Now, imagine God's sovereignty as being like a Scrabble game. But instead of only seven letters, God has an infinite number of them. And instead of one board limited to a 15-by-15 grid, God has an infinite number of boards of infinite size, filling every plane of the universe. In one move God could play every piece on every square of every board, and no matter which angle you looked at, it spelled a word — infinitely. In a small way, that's similar to what's happening in God's "control room."

But on our side of the equation, we're very limited in understanding. As Sinclair Ferguson says, "What is plain to him is frequently obscure to us."[11] Our perspective is small and our capacity for calculating the relationships between every situation in the past, present, and future is almost nonexistent. Our speculation over God's will in just one circumstance or feeling or thought is at best a shot in the dark without the solid evidence of God's Word.

Pray the Word

One of the chief ways God's Word shapes and guides us is through prayer. Consider the example of prayer that Jesus gave His disciples:

> Our Father in heaven,
> hallowed be your name.
> Your kingdom come,
> *your will be done*,
>   on earth as it is in heaven.
> Give us this day our daily bread,
> and forgive us our debts,
>   as we also have forgiven our debtors.
> And lead us not into temptation,
>   but deliver us from evil (Matthew 6:9-13).

Every line of this model prayer from Jesus is based upon what Scripture declares; none of it was "new" revelation. Consider the Scriptural basis for each line of the prayer:

Our Father in heaven — "Our God is in the heavens; he does all that he pleases" (Psalm 115:3).

Hallowed be your name — "Ascribe to the LORD the glory due his name" (Psalm 29:2).

Your kingdom come, your will be done, on earth as it is in heaven — "The LORD has established his throne in the heavens, and his kingdom rules over all" (Psalm 103:19).

Give us this day our daily bread — "The eyes of all look to you, and you give them their food in due season" (Psalm 145:15).

Forgive us our debts, as we also have forgiven our debtors — "Consider my affliction and my trouble, and forgive all my sins" (Psalm 25:18).

Lead us not into temptation, but deliver us from evil — "He leads me in paths of righteousness for his name's sake" (Psalm 23:3).

Note that here and elsewhere in the Gospels,

we don't see Jesus praying like this: "Father, show Peter which new boat he should buy, and give Nathaniel a peace about which donkey to purchase." Instead, the keynote of His prayer life is this core request: "Your will be done" (see also Matthew 26:39, 42; John 4:34; 5:30; 6:38).

Don't misunderstand; praying for God's will to be done doesn't mean we never express our feelings before God. In fact, this is a great way to open our hearts before God and survey our desires in comparison with His Word. Discussing our desires before God is an excellent practice to clarify our intentions and make sure they're in line with Scripture. That's exactly what Jesus did in the Garden of Gethsemane when He prayed, *"Father, if you are willing, remove this cup from me."* And then He immediately affirmed, *"Nevertheless, not my will, but yours, be done"* (Luke 22:42).

I find it helpful to express to God what it is that I desire, and then to add, "But more than anything, I want your will to be done."

God is pleased when we pray about every detail of our life. But our prayers shouldn't be haphazard and random. Instead, they should be discussions of how our desires can conform to God's desires revealed in Scripture. Instead of seeking more inside information from God's control room, we should seek the things He has commanded us to seek in His manual — the Bible.

What to Pray For

When we pray God's Word, we can be confident God will answer, as the teaching of Jesus again affirms:

Ask, and it will be given to you; seek, and you will find; knock, and it will be opened to you. For everyone who asks receives, and the one who seeks finds, and to the one who knocks it will be opened. Or which one of you, if his son asks him for bread, will give him a stone? Or if he asks for a fish, will give him a serpent? If you then, who are evil, know how to give good gifts to your children, how much more will your Father who is in heaven give good things to those who ask him! (Matthew 7:7-11).

If God is eager to *"give good things to those*

who ask him," the only question is, What should we ask for?

We know the answer is *not* "anything we dream up." The words in James 4:3 exposes our sinful tendency here: *"You ask wrongly, to spend it on your passions."* Instead we must pray for what God has already told us He desires for us, so that *His* desires become *our* desires.

For example, we know God wants us to exhibit the fruit of the Spirit; therefore we can confidently pray for *"love, joy, peace, patience, kindness, goodness, faithfulness, gentleness,* [and] *self-control"* (Galatians 5:22-23), knowing God desires those things for us.

Similarly, we understand that God calls us to "love our neighbor as ourselves" (Matthew 22:39). So we can be confident in asking God to help us be more sensitive to the needs of others.

Because we know that *"God opposes the proud, but gives grace to the humble"* (James 4:6), we can ask God to help us resist pride, knowing He shares this same desire for us. And of course, the list of God's desires for us as revealed in Scripture could go on and on.

Has a friend betrayed you? Pray that God will help you *"repay no one evil for evil, but give thought to do what is honorable in the sight of all"* (Romans 12:17). Has your child misbehaved? Pray for strength to *"train up a child in the way he should go"* (Proverbs 22:6), while remembering to *"not provoke your children to anger"* (Ephesians 6:4). Is money tight this month? Ask God to help you seek first His kingdom and His righteousness (Matthew 6:33) and to be content in every situation (Philippians 4:11).

Think of all the things you can request with confidence! It's just a matter of asking in accordance with Scripture! Then we continually receive the guidance we long for.

Jensen and Payne express it this way: "Many of our problems with guidance stem from precisely this: we ask the wrong questions.... We should ask the questions that God thinks are important, and these are the questions he has answered in the Bible."[12]

As we pray His Word consistently, He begins to conform our heart to His Word. Imagine taking time daily to pray, "God help me love my neighbor as myself." After praying this for months, how do you think you might react when you see an elderly man's yard in your neighborhood that needs mowing?

Prayer doesn't change God — it changes *us*.

NOTES

1. Robinson, 15-16.

2. Robinson, 15-16.

3. Martin Luther, *The Bondage of the Will*, translated by J. I. Packer & O. R. Johnston (Grand Rapids, Michigan: Revell, 1999), 170-171.

4. Wayne Grudem and Elliot Grudem, ed., *Christian Beliefs* (Grand Rapids, Michigan: Zondervan, 2005), 19.

5. Jonathan Edwards, *Thoughts on the Revival of Religion in New England*, Section II: "Wrong Principles," vol. 1 in *Works of Jonathan Edwards* (Bath, England: The Bath Press, 1974), 404.

6. Phillip Jensen and Tony Payne, *Guidance and the Voice of God* (Kingsford, New South Wales, Australia: Mathias Media, 2005), 95-96.

7. Jensen and Payne, 89.

8. Jay Adams, *A Theology of Christian Counseling* (Grand Rapids, Michigan: Zondervan, 1979), 26.

9. Michael A. G. Haykin, *The Revived Puritan: The*

Spirituality of George Whitefield (Dundas, Ontario, Canada: Joshua Press, 2000), 167-170.

10. R. C. Sproul, *Chosen By God* (Carol Stream, Illinois: Tyndale House, 1994), 26-27.

11. Sinclair Ferguson, *Discovering God's Will* (Carlisle, Pennsylvania: Banner of Truth Trust, 2001), 32.

12. Jensen and Payne, 101.

GOD'S WILL IS IN WISDOM

The apostle Peter tells us that God's *"divine power has granted to us all things that pertain to life and godliness"* (2 Peter 1:3). By *"all things,"* he means everything we need to live in godliness (God's will). And in the same passage, Peter makes it clear this promise is fulfilled through the sufficiency of Scripture.

You might object: "*All* things? How can that be? I can't find any cross references in my Bible for *choosing a career, buying a new home,* or *finding a spouse.*"

The answer lies in the place where understanding meets wisdom. We *understand* God's Word through the careful, constant study of Scripture. We learn how to live out God's will by practicing the *wisdom* God provides. Navigation skills are only sharpened by consistent interaction with trustworthy directions.

Get Wisdom

Much of the book of Proverbs was written by the wisest man in history, King Solomon, as a tool to disciple his son. Listen to his advice: *"Incline your ear to wisdom, and apply your heart to understanding.... For the LORD gives wisdom; from His mouth come knowledge and understanding"* (Proverbs 2:2, 6, NKJV)[1]; *"Blessed is the one who finds wisdom, and the one who gets understanding"* (Proverbs 3:13). Yet nowhere in this book of advice does Solomon tell his son, "Try to figure out God's specific plan for your life."

In *Just Do Something*, Kevin DeYoung comments on this:

> Isn't it interesting that we are never told in Scripture to ask God to reveal the future or to show us His plan for our lives? But we are

told — in no uncertain terms — to call out for insight and to cry aloud for understanding. In other words, God says, "Don't ask to see all the plans I've made for you. Ask Me for wisdom so you'll know how to live according to My Book."[2]

Haddon Robinson addresses this as well:

We must face the fact: "How do you know the will of God in making life's decisions?" is not a biblical question! The Bible never tells us to ask it. The Bible never gives us direction in answering it. And the pursuit of some personalized version of the "will of God" often leads us toward disobedience. When we find ourselves facing the tough choices in life — those day-in, day-out decisions which make up the very fabric of our existence — we shouldn't seek special messages from God. Instead, we should ask, "How do we develop the skills necessary to make wise and prudent choices?" The Bible does speak to that question — at length. We should not turn to Scripture in search of a detailed road map. The Bible is not so much a map as it is a compass. It doesn't give us specifics, but it does provide direction.[3]

And the very wisdom we need in *applying* God's Word is *supplied* in God's Word.

The Psalmist understood this concept:

> Oh how I love your law!
>   It is my meditation all the day.
> *Your commandment makes me wiser* than my
>   enemies,
>   for it is ever with me.
> *I have more understanding* than all my teachers,
>   for your testimonies are my meditation.
> *I understand more* than the aged,
>   for I keep your precepts.
> I hold back my feet from every evil way,
>   in order to keep your word.
> I do not turn aside from your rules,
>   for you have taught me.
> How sweet are your words to my taste,
>   sweeter than honey to my mouth!
> *Through your precepts I get understanding*;
>   therefore I hate every false way
>   (Psalm 119:97-104).[4]

Wow! The Psalmist was passionate about being transformed by *God's Word* to live out *God's will* through *God's wisdom*!

Maybe you have a difficult time exercising wisdom in applying God's Word to life situations. We all do from time to time. That's why God calls us to seek wise counsel: *"Whoever walks with the wise becomes wise"* (Proverbs 13:20); *"Listen to advice and accept instruction, that you may gain wisdom in the future"* (Proverbs 19:20).

Likewise, one of the most repeated instructions given in Scripture is to pray for wisdom. In fact, God even promises, *"If any of you lacks wisdom, let him ask God, who gives generously to all without reproach, and it will be given him"* (James 1:5-6).

Jesus Didn't Do Career Counseling

Perhaps the greatest argument for making decisions based upon wisdom lies in the example of Christ.

If God desired for everyone to receive special revelation about life's most important decisions, surely their career would be worthy of such revelation — and the Son of God would be the prime candidate to deliver it. However, we have no record of Jesus ever consulting with anyone regarding where they should work. (For that matter, we have no record of Christ matchmaking either.) Simply put, Jesus didn't do career counseling.

But He did give plenty of instruction on character and godliness. It seems He was much more interested in *how* a person worked than *where* a person worked. He was more concerned that a man become a godly husband than that he find the perfect wife.

So how did Jesus expect people to land the right job or marry the right person? Through *wisdom*.

After all, isn't it hypocritical to want special revelation about certain "big" decisions (large purchases, college majors, family relocations) while we ignore biblical revelation in the rest of life? Why do we want to know where we'll end up, when we aren't concerned with who we'll be when we get there?

It's like we want God to tell us our ultimate

destination so we can ditch His direction and find our own way there. But this misses an important point: God has ordained not only our destination, but also the means by which we'll get there. That's why He's pleased when we obey His Word and trust Him with every decision, knowing He's always guiding us — even though we don't fully understand how.

When the apostles instructed the early church to choose seven men to be the first deacons, they didn't say, "Ask God to lead you to the right men for this office." Instead they simply said, *"Pick out from among you seven men of good repute, full of the Spirit and of wisdom, whom we will appoint to this duty"* (Acts 6:3). They expected the people to make wise decisions based on scriptural standards.

Special Guidance From God in the Book of Acts

But aren't there instances in the book of Acts where God gives special revelation? Of course — but not as many as you might suppose. Further, Scripture never calls us to pursue such revelation, and the apostles themselves didn't seek it out.

Paul's call to go to Macedonia is a great example. Paul was on his way to visit churches he'd established on his first missionary journey when he received a vision of a man from Macedonia saying, "Come help us." Immediately, he changed course and went to Macedonia.

Notice a couple of key facts about this case. First, Paul and his companions weren't sitting around "waiting to hear the voice of God" to determine where to go next. They went where they thought best. According to all indications, exercising wisdom was the normal practice of all the apostles. Rarely did God interrupt their plans with special revelation.

Notice also in this Macedonian situation that when God speaks, it's unmistakable. Paul didn't have to question, wonder, or doubt the message. When God communicates, He's loud and clear.

Two other examples of special revelation in Acts include the Lord's guiding Philip to an encounter with the Ethiopian eunuch (Acts 8:26) and His guiding Cornelius to invite Peter into his home (Acts 10:1-6). These reinforce the principles we see in Paul's experience with the Macedonian vision, as Haddon Robinson points out:

> In all these occasions reported in Acts, God speaks to people who are not looking for leading, not specifically trying to find God's will. He speaks at times when He desires a major change in the church's direction. And when He speaks He does not give His hearers a holy hunch or some kind of inner feeling. There is an unambiguous divine voice.[5]

The apostles' example teaches us to be confident in making decisions based upon wisdom — knowing that God can easily get your attention if He needs to change your plans.

What About a "Fleece"?

So what about the concept of "putting out a fleece"? This refers of course to the example of Gideon in Judges 6, where God appears and tells him to lead the army of Israel against the Midianites. Gideon has trouble accepting the message, so he lays out a wool fleece and asks God to confirm the message by making the fleece wet with dew while the ground remains dry. The next morning, God had obliged Gideon's request.

But that wasn't enough for Gideon. He laid the fleece out a second time and asked God for another sign. This time, Gideon asked for the fleece to be dry and the ground to be wet. Once again, God granted his request.

Notice two things about this story. First, it starts with God speaking to Gideon in a clear, unambiguous way. When most people talk about "putting out a fleece," they start with their own idea — not God's. This reduces their "fleece" to nothing more than wanting God to be their Magic 8-Ball.

Second, Gideon's fleece was evidence of a lack of trust in God, since he had already heard God clearly. Gideon never questioned the content of God's message, but only whether it was true. In granting the confirmation that Gideon sought, God was displaying great patience and mercy toward Gideon.

So if you really want to "put out a fleece" in the biblical sense, you must start with God's Word, something He has already clearly stated — for example, the Great Commission in Matthew 28:18-20. Then, while clearly understanding the passage's content, you must question its truth. You might say, "God, I understand your command that we should make disciples of all nations, but I want you to do something miraculous to prove that you really mean it." That's the gist of what Gideon was doing.

Haddon Robinson relates a conversation with a seminary student:

> She told me she was thinking of going skiing, but she was seeking the mind of God as to whether or not she ought to go. I asked her how she expected to determine God's will on the matter. Very matter-of-factly she said, "Well, I put out a fleece. If my daddy sends me some money, then I'll know that skiing is something God wants me to do.

The student hadn't grasped the weight of Gideon's request. After all, her father sent money often. It wouldn't have been strange to receive a check at any time.

So Robinson encouraged her:

If you're really going to put out a fleece, why not a good one? After all, if you go skiing and you're not in God's will, you might break your neck. Why don't you pray that the president will send you a letter, and in that letter there will be a check that will give you enough to go skiing? And if you're really going to follow Gideon's example to the limit, pray that you get a second letter and a check from Britain's prime minister the next day. When you get both checks, back-to-back, you can be assured that God wants you to go skiing. That's the type of miraculous sign that Gideon wanted from God. His odds weren't 70-30; he was asking for two miracles, and he got them both![6]

In your own situation, even if the "fleece" you're requesting is a clearly miraculous sign, be aware that just because God acted in such ways in the past doesn't mean we should expect Him to do the same now (Hebrews 1:1-2). After all, the practice of casting lots is found in Scripture, but I don't see a lot of churches making staffing decisions by rolling dice!

What About "The Call"?

I've always found it strange that when asked to describe their "call to the ministry," most pastors have a hard time speaking clearly. They seem to struggle with this question and talk in circles — almost as if they're still trying to figure it out themselves. But should we expect anything else from a subjective feeling?

Let me share my unpopular view. It's really simple: *A call to salvation is a call to ministry.* Period. That's it.

And it's easy to explain. Here's the biblical reasoning. The New Testament doesn't speak about "being called" to be a pastor or missionary. It does, however, speak of a calling to salvation and holy living. Here are a few examples:

"I came not to call the righteous, but sinners" (Matthew 9:13).

"We know that for those who love God all things work together for good, for those who are called according to his purpose" (Romans 8:28).

"God has not called us for impurity, but in holiness" (1 Thessalonians 4:7).

"You are a chosen race, a royal priesthood, a holy nation, a people for his own possession, that you may proclaim the excellencies of him who called you out of darkness into his marvelous light" (1 Peter 2:9).

So what does God's Word say to a man who's thinking about being a pastor? "The saying is trustworthy: *"If anyone aspires to the office of overseer, he desires a noble task"* (1 Timothy 3:1). Does that desire come from God? Yes!

I think this *desire* is what most men are sincerely describing when they talk about a "call." But talking about a subjective feeling as if it's a matter of fact can breed confusion for others struggling with the issue. It's as if those inside the "ministry club" are saying, "We all know the secret handshake; do you?" So prospective pastors and missionaries are nervously thinking, "Maybe I do, but I can't be sure unless someone shows it to me — and every time I ask about it, they talk in circles and sound confused!"

This idea of a specialized call to ministry also has the potential to distract men from the rest of 1 Timothy 3, which emphasizes the biblical qualifications for ministry leadership. What a tragedy for men to mistake the normal feelings toward ministry that every believer should have and interpret them instead as a special divine "call" to be a pastor, when they haven't even contemplated whether they're actually qualified for ministry leadership. It can become an attempt to deal with God's secret work behind the scenes while ignoring our responsibility to His Word.

No wonder pastors who buy into such an idea have a hard time describing "the call"; they're trying to understand what only God can fathom! Don't we trust God to take His Word, plus the gifts and desires He's given us, and to work behind the scenes through the circumstances of our decision-making to accomplish exactly what He wants us to do? If we have no problem believing God ordains the desired outcome, why do we have a problem believing He's also in control of the means for getting there? Is it because such a process involves the decisions that happen inside our brain? Do we think our decision-making will somehow defeat God's sovereignty? As if God would say, "I didn't see that one coming!"

Think about the prophecy of Malachi concerning John the Baptist: *"Behold, I send my messenger, and he will prepare the way before me"* (Malachi 3:1). God seems pretty confident that John the Baptist will fulfill his purpose without "falling off the tightrope" of His will or "missing the bull's-eye." I'm not saying John the Baptist was a robot without a will; I'm saying God's sovereignty is so big that human decisions are a part of His plan that will not be thwarted.

Now, why is it fairly easy for us to believe God was sovereign over every decision John the Baptist made — but we struggle to believe His sovereignty over our own decision-making? After all, isn't that what we're asking God to do for others when we pray, "Change Brian's heart," or, "Keep Jenny safe on the road"?

Have you forgotten that God is sovereign over both triumphs and failures, and both righteousness and sin? Only a perfectly wise and powerful God could use the selling of Joseph into slavery by his brothers, the hardening of Pharaoh's heart, the death of Ruth's husband, and the slavery of His children to Babylon as part of His eternal plan for

His people. How amazing is our God!

As Peter preached on the day of Pentecost, he told the crowd in Jerusalem, *"This Jesus, delivered up according to the definite plan and foreknowledge of God, you crucified and killed by the hands of lawless men"* (Acts 2:23). If the most sinful act of history could also be a part of God's "definite plan," surely He's also sovereign over your failures and sin as well.

Some may argue that God's use of our sin actually makes him guilty for our sin. But just the opposite is true. The fact that God can use *anything* for His purposes — including our sin — reflects the all-surpassing greatness of His power. At the same time, God's sovereignty over our weaknesses and mistakes and sins doesn't relieve us from our responsibility for them.

Imagine the scene: Just as Satan is starting to boast over your sin, he realizes, once again, that God is using it for His glory. No matter how great Satan's influence, God's power always overcomes evil with good.

Edith Schaeffer's book *The Tapestry* is the story of her own life and that of her husband, Francis

Schaeffer. It portrays how the decisions, events, tragedies, and triumphs of all our lives are woven together as threads within a divine tapestry.[7] Occasionally, from our vantage point on this side of eternity, we might see patterns emerge and make sense of a few stitches. But our perspective is much too small to see the "big picture." And even if we could see the entire tapestry, we can still see only the back of it — the "earth" side of it — full of knots and loose threads.

Imagine the coming day, however, when we pass from this life to the next and begin to gaze in full upon the front of the tapestry, the "heaven" side of it. We'll recognize how all the decisions we made, the paths we followed, and the situations we encountered were designed together to produce a beautiful picture of God's divine sovereignty and wisdom.

Wisdom trusts that through all the knots and tangles of life, God is weaving a masterpiece.

Wise Questions for Navigating Decisions

So how do we make wise decisions? Here are some questions to ask in your times of decision:

What does Scripture say? This should be our first pursuit. If Scripture speaks directly to your issue (Should I seek to hurt someone who's hurt me? Can I distort the facts on my résumé to help me get a better job? Should I join my friends in gossiping about a coworker?) then that should be the end of the decision-making process. Of course, Scripture may be silent on your particular issue. But there are always *principles* in Scripture that apply to our every situation, and we must seek in wisdom to identify these.

What should I pray? When Scripture speaks directly to an issue, I don't need to pray about *what* to do, but instead for *strength* to do it. For example, I know I must love my neighbor whose dog keeps digging holes in my yard (Matthew 22:39). I just need the grace of Christ to do so.

When the Word doesn't address my issue directly, but provides principles related to my issue, I must pray for wisdom (Proverbs 4:5). Remember, God *wants* to give us wisdom — so pray boldly. Lay out the situation before Him, with all the details, emotions, and possibilities. Ask Him to help you make a Christlike decision.

What are my gifts? Wisdom will take into account how God has gifted us to serve in His kingdom. To be a pastor, the Bible says a man must have the gift of teaching (2 Timothy 2:24). But for other roles, gifts aren't necessarily required so much as they are useful (Romans 12:3-6; 1 Corinthians 12; Ephesians 4:11-14).

A wise person will want to find ways to use the gifts God has given him. Of course, we can't use the lack of a certain gift as an excuse to disobey God's Word. Just because I don't have the gift of evangelism doesn't mean I'm exempt from the Great Commission.

What do I desire? Along with gifts, the wise person will contemplate what he truly longs for. Remember, not all desires are from God (James 1:14; 2 Corinthians 11:14). That's why I would suggest not dealing with this question until you've already worked through the question of what God's Word says.

If you have a desire for something God desires (serving the poor, teaching the Bible, etc.), you should use wisdom in determining how to pursue it.

If you have a desire for something Scripture is silent about and doesn't forbid — just do what you want to do! But such truly "neutral" decisions are more rare than you might think, especially considering the relational factors that are typically involved, and the extensiveness of biblical teaching on loving and serving others. For example, there's no shortage of opportunities for practicing the biblical principle to think of others more highly than yourself (Philippians 2:3). While you have biblical freedom to do what you want, it never overrules the equally biblical imperative to live out the kind of love that *"does not insist on its own way"* (1 Corinthians 13:5). As Paul also says, *"Do not use your freedom as an opportunity for the flesh, but through love serve one another"* (Galatians 5:13).

Should I seek counsel? It's not uncommon for Christians to become overwhelmed when trying to determine what (if anything) the Bible says about an issue, or how to put their decision into perspective with their gifts and desires. In those situations, we need to consider seeking counsel. But it's important to get *wise* counsel (Proverbs

1:5). Find a believer who makes good biblical decisions and has walked with the Lord for a long time. Explain your issue, and ask them for insight.

NOTES

1. Scripture taken from the New King James Version®. Copyright © 1982 by Thomas Nelson, Inc. Used by permission. All rights reserved.

2. Kevin DeYoung, *Just Do Something* (Chicago, Illinois: Moody, 2009), 90.

3. Robinson, 61.

4. *Italics* in these Scripture quotations are the author's emphasis.

5. Robinson, 135.

6. Robinson, 30-31.

7. Edith Schaeffer, *The Tapestry* (Waco, Texas: Word Books, 1981).

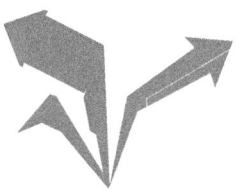

GOD'S WILL IS IN WORSHIP

One of my favorite passages about God's will is found in Romans 12:1-2.

I appeal to you therefore, brothers, by the mercies of God, to present your bodies as a living sacrifice, holy and acceptable to God, which is your spiritual worship. Do not be conformed to this world, but be transformed by the renewal of your mind, that by testing you may discern what is the will of God, what is good and acceptable and perfect.

Let's break down these verses.

It Takes Effort to Navigate Life

At the end of these verses, we see where Paul is heading. He's out to explain how to discern the will of God. And he says that we understand God's will in our life by "testing."

Does that mean he's calling for a "trial and error" method? No, he's describing the process of testing our decisions by Scripture and being shaped by Scripture. Notice the use of the word *"discern"* instead of *listen* or *feel*. Testing Scripture requires using our brain. That's why Paul insists here that we not be conformed to this world, but that we be transformed by renewing our mind. It's a process that depends on the illumination of the Holy Spirit, on prayer, and oftentimes on wise counsel regarding Scripture.

Meanwhile, as we "test" our decisions by Scripture, we're confident that God is working through various means behind the scenes to accomplish His purpose.

Notice also here that Paul equates the will of God with *"what is good and acceptable and perfect."* Living in God's will is synonymous with pleasing God, exercising faith, and growing in Christlikeness.

A Lifestyle of Navigation

We see also in this passage that walking in God's will means a life of worship. Using imagery of the Old Testament sacrificial system, Paul draws a comparison: *"Present your bodies as a living sacrifice."* Our worship is to be practical and thorough. God doesn't just ask for our hearts; He asks for all of us — for our hands, feet, eyes, mouths, and everything else. We worship God with all that we are, and we do so not as a dead sacrifice, but *living*! Worship is our *life*style.

That's why Paul calls it our *"spiritual worship."* Recall the conversation Jesus had with the woman at the well, and how He told her that one day people would not worship on one mountain or the other, but instead would worship *"in spirit and truth"* (John 4:21-23). Jesus was explaining that worship isn't confined to a location like a church auditorium or summer-camp tabernacle. Worship should happen everywhere a believer goes — at home, at work, in class, on the lake, around the golf course, in the shopping mall, or at the ballgame.

And that lifestyle should be *"holy and acceptable"* — something that pleases God and glorifies Him, all the time, everywhere we go.

So the will of God *is* worship. Likewise, worship is God's will. God desires for you to live a lifestyle that honors Him, and that equates to worship. It rises up as a sweet fragrance to God, just like the scent of the old sacrifices (Leviticus 1:9; 2 Corinthians 2:15).

Call to Worship

Recall again Paul's opening words in Romans 12, where he says, "I appeal to you *therefore…*" Paul is now drawing conclusions based upon everything he has already stated up to this point in his letter — eleven detailed chapters focused on salvation, or, as he expresses it in 12:1, *"the mercies of God."*

Our ultimate goal is not to merely *know* God's will, *interpret* God's will, or *understand* God's will. Instead, we are called to *live* God's will.

Living God's will is an overflow of our salvation. It's fueled by the active work of Christ in our hearts. In the most simple of terms, living God's will means Christlike living. And it's lived out practically through the gifts God has given us as we obey His Word and follow His example. That's what the rest of Romans 12 is all about.

Let's explore what this could look like in our lives.

Living God's Will

Kasey has two months before high school graduation, and she has narrowed down her college choice to two schools. Both schools are strong academically and offer the degree Kasey is seeking. How will she decide where to go?

As she thinks about what Scripture has to say, Kasey recalls Hebrews 10:24-25: *"Let us consider how to stir up one another to love and good works, not neglecting to meet together, as is the habit of some, but encouraging one another."* God desires all believers to be active in a local church where godly relationships will encourage them and help them grow. After researching local churches around both campuses, Kasey finds a church where she believes she'll have the most opportunity to connect with other growing Christians her age, where the sermons are biblical, and where the people place an emphasis on serving the community together.

After praying for God to help her make a wise decision, Kasey chooses her college destination based upon her biblical desire to be part of a strong local church. She's convinced her spiritual growth over the next four years will be more valuable than her academic growth. At the same time, her spiritual growth will stimulate her academic growth (1 Corinthians 10:31).

***

Jill has a new job offer. She likes her present position and working environment a great deal, but the new one would pay more money for doing essentially the same tasks. What should she do? Scripturally, she can find nothing wrong with either job. Both are ethically acceptable, and neither would take more time away from family than the other.

She asks God to give her wisdom and help her

decide which job will provide the best opportunity to show the love of Christ to others. After several days of praying, both jobs still seem equal. Both have plenty of opportunities to serve others for the sake of the gospel.

Jill schedules an appointment to talk with her pastor. After explaining the situation, she asks if he sees any other issues that should be considered. Jill's pastor can't think of anything else and suggests that she choose the job she desires most.

The next day, Jill declined the new job offer. She considers herself blessed to already have a job and workplace she loves, and she doesn't want to risk a new situation which she might end up not enjoying quite as well — even with more pay.

***

Ben and Kristen have become serious in their relationship. How does Ben decide whether to ask Kristen to marry him?

He knows Kristen is a godly young lady. That's what attracted him to her in the first place. And over the past two years of dating, he has grown to love her family.

But he's also acquainted with other single godly women. Why should Kristen be the particular one he marries?

After praying for wisdom in the matter, Ben makes a list of reasons for marrying Kristen and shares it with his parents. The list includes mutual interests, ability to communicate well, their history of conflict resolution, and personal attraction. (The list also has some mushy parts, but we'll leave those out.) Both Ben and his parents agree that Kristen is a great match.

Finally, Ben concludes that marrying Kristen is a wise decision. Fortunately, Kristen agrees!

***

Keri is up late working on her personal income tax return. She discovers a way to reduce her payment this year by claiming false deductions.

As the idea crosses her mind, she thinks about Exodus 20:15: *"You shall not steal."* She also remembers the words of Jesus: *"Render to Caesar the things that are Caesar's"* (Matthew 22:21).

Immediately she makes her decision, followed by a prayer: "Father, help me stay true to my decision not to steal from the government. I want to obey you."

***

Bryce has been thinking about becoming a missionary in India. What should his decision-making process look like?

He knows that God desires believers to make disciples in all nations (Matthew 28:18-20) through the preaching of the gospel (Romans 10:14-15). Further, he has a strong desire to share the gospel with people from India. In fact, he has discipled several of his Indian friends in college who have come to Christ.

His campus minister believes Bryce has a gift for teaching, and together they review the list of pastoral qualifications in 1 Timothy 3. Bryce admits to the minister that he struggles with one of the qualifications: self-control. From time to time, he lashes out when things don't go his way.

His campus minister suggests that Bryce continue pursuing his desire to be a missionary, but not to go immediately. Bryce agrees. He'll begin praying for God to change his heart and help him exercise self-control. In the meantime, he'll begin taking a missions course online to prepare for the future.

***

Ed and Nancy receive an inheritance check in the mail from Ed's uncle. What should they do with all the money?

Nancy isn't sure if they should tithe from it. Ed isn't sure either, but in his opinion it's better to do so even if it isn't required. After all, it's not as if God will penalize them for their generosity! Nancy agrees. But that still leaves a lot left over. The couple has no debt and no plans to move. In fact, they aren't really lacking for anything.

After searching through numerous passages in the Bible concerning money, Nancy comes to a realization: Scripture consistently affirms generous giving, and it never condones hoarding or greed. Ed and Nancy decide they'll find ways to give away the money to bless others in their church. They give half of the money to an infertile couple saving for adoption, and the other half to a summer mission team.

After the summer mission trip, you can guess who was sitting on the edge of their seats waiting to hear about the trip — as well as who found special joy each time they saw the adopted little girl laughing with her new parents. Ed and Nancy were experiencing this truth: *"It is more blessed to give than to receive"* (Acts 20:35).

***

The scenarios above aren't meant to reflect legalistic guidelines. Ed and Nancy would not have been sinning if they'd decided to buy an RV with their inheritance money. And who's to say Kasey couldn't have honored God at the other university? It's definitely possible that Jill could have been happy and fulfilled at the other job, and that Ben could have loved and married a different young lady. For that matter, Bryce could have decided to honor God as a real estate agent rather than as a missionary.

But the bigger issue is that all these persons made decisions with a desire to honor God to the best of their ability, while trusting Him to guide every move according to His divine plan. That is *worship*; that is the will of God.

Every decision you make to navigate life can be an act of worship as you test and approve God's will. The choice to spend time with a hurting friend is an act of worship when it springs from a desire to obey Christ's command to *"love one another"* (John 13:34). The decision to end a romantic relationship because the young man isn't a believer (2 Corinthians 6:14) is a sweet fragrance to God. Taking an extra shift each week to make sure a child with special needs receives therapy (1 Timothy 5:8) is living as a sacrifice, holy and pleasing to God.

So go ahead — enjoy freedom from confusing feelings and misunderstood circumstances as you navigate the will of God. Offer your bodies as living sacrifices by the way you study for tests, respect your boss, interact with your neighbors, romance your wife, and raise your children. Live out God's will through a lifestyle of worship by pursuing wisdom and by growing in God's Word.

A Delightful Path to Navigate

Navigating God's will is more than possible — it's meant to be the normal Christian life. God isn't playing an eternal game of hide-and-seek with you. His will is clearly printed in the pages of Scripture for those who have *"ears to hear"* (Mark 4:9).

Like the Psalmist, may you say with all your heart, *"Lead me in the path of your commandments, for I delight in it"* (Psalm 119:35).

Recommended Reading

Hopefully this brief book has stimulated your curiosity and brought questions to your mind. Here are three books I would highly recommend on the subject of God's will, each of them addressing a wider scope of issues in greater detail:

- *Just Do Something* by Kevin DeYoung
- *Guidance and the Voice of God* by Phillip Jensen and Tony Payne
- *Decision-Making by the Book* by Haddon Robinson

www.ingramcontent.com/pod-product-compliance
Lightning Source LLC
Chambersburg PA
CBHW052029290426
44112CB00014B/2433